MAGIC MONSTERS
Learn About Safety

by Sylvia Root Tester
illustrated by Helen Endres

THE CHILD'S WORLD

ELGIN, ILLINOIS 60120

Sammy had two pets, magic monster pets. He was afraid his pets might hurt someone. So Sammy said, "I'll have to teach you the safe way to do things. You're just too big to be dangerous."

Here's what Sammy told his pets: "Watch how people obey safety rules. People are careful with fire."

Strike match away from body.

Hold match so it won't burn fingers.

Be sure match is out.

Watch pans
on stove.

Don't play with fire.

Keep back
from campfire.

Sammy added, "Magic monsters need two
more rules. . .

Be careful when you open your mouth!

And be careful where you stand!

''People learn to be careful with sharp things.

Watch out for fingers.

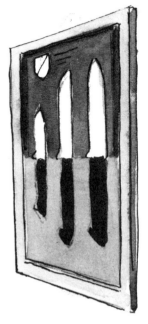

Put knives away carefully.

Carry scissors
like this.

Use scissors carefully.

"Magic monsters also need rules about
using sharp things. . .

Be careful with your claws!

And be careful **with your teeth!**

"People are careful when they walk. They follow safety rules.

Obey walk signals.

Obey traffic lights.

Obey the crossing guard.

14

If there is no sidewalk,
walk facing traffic.

Never go off
with strangers.

"When magic monsters go out walking
and flying, there are two more rules. . .

Be careful where you step!

And be careful
where you land!

17

"People obey playground rules.

Walk way
around swings.

Stop at the curb
if ball goes in street.

18

Be careful when running so you won't run into anyone or fall.

Climb carefully.

"When magic monsters play, there is one more rule. . .

Play gently!

21

''People obey all of the water rules.

Walk, don't run.

Play gently.

Take turns.

"Magic monsters have one special rule. . .

23

Swim in the ocean instead!

"People are careful in houses.

Watch babies carefully.

Be careful with electricity.

Be careful with hot irons.

Pick up toys on stairs, so people will not fall.

Don't touch poisons.

"For magic monsters, there is just one house rule. . .

Stay outside!''

Sammy had two magic monster pets.
Sammy obeyed all the people rules. And his
pets obeyed all the magic monster rules.

And so they all lived together very
happily indeed.